telephone
skills

PATRICK FORSYTH

INSTITUTE OF PERSONNEL AND DEVELOPMENT

First published in the *Training Extras* series in 1997
First published in the *Management Shapers* series in 2000

Design by Curve
Typesetting by Paperweight
Printed in Great Britain by
The Guernsey Press, Channel Islands

British Library Cataloguing in Publication Data
A catalogue record for this book is available from the
British Library

ISBN
0-85292-865-3

The views expressed in this book are the author's own and
may not necessarily reflect those of the IPD.

**INSTITUTE OF PERSONNEL
AND DEVELOPMENT**

IPD House, Camp Road, London SW19 4UX
Tel.: 020-8971 9000   Fax: 020-8263 3333
Registered office as above. Registered Charity No. 1038333.
A company limited by guarantee. Registered in England No. 2931892.

contents

Other titles in the series:

introduction: something I said?

Well, if I called the wrong number, why did you answer the telephone?

James Thurber

It is something you recognise instantly: 'Er, yes…hold on – Sorry, will you repeat that? – Well, it's a bit difficult, y'know. Just a tick.' It is the 'abominable no-man' of the telephone, the moment when, even after only a few words, you *know* the communication is going to be difficult. Yet the reverse is true, too. Some people, also within a few words, create confidence. They make you feel that all will be well, that a good start has been made, and they get you looking forward to what comes next.

The telephone is ubiquitous and has of course been around a long time. It now comes not only as a simple piece of equipment but as part of a profusion of electronic wizardry that can store information, carry out umpteen functions at once, and play music if you are kept waiting. It may be digital and portable. Life may be unimaginable without it, but it should not be taken for granted. Good telephone communication does not just happen. It needs thinking about. It needs planning, and communication by telephone needs executing with care.

Why? Because it is a powerful medium. The telephone can create a strong, perhaps lasting, impression – and do so for good or ill. It can typecast the speaker and his or her organisation as efficient, helpful, positive, and more, or set him or her apart as an off-putting representative of an uncaring corporate dinosaur. This is possible at all levels and in all ways: the switchboard, someone dealing with a colleague in another department, external contact with customers we want to impress, or suppliers on whose goodwill we are dependent. All such communications are influenced by telephone manner and thus by telephone skills.

Hence this publication. There are principles and techniques involved that, properly deployed, can make this a major opportunity for improved communications and better image-building. If everyone in an organisation has been well briefed, understands the difference that can be made, and uses the techniques consciously to create an impact that is appropriate, then the benefits can be considerable. Good telephone technique can:

- create an appropriate and positive image

- avoid communications breakdown and thus delay, confusion, and perhaps waste of time and money

- smooth the whole communications process on which any organisation is dependent, internally and externally.

An inherent fragility

Not only is it important to get telephone contact right, there is more to it than a simple resolve to speak carefully. The process is inherently fragile: that is, small differences along the way can make a major difference to the overall effect.

One example I experienced that well illustrates this point occurred as I waited in the reception area of a company, having arrived a few minutes early for a meeting. The receptionist also staffed the switchboard, and it quickly became apparent that she was very busy. Calls seemed to come in every few seconds and the majority were, clearly, from customers. The company had two separate departments that were predominantly concerned with customer contact: a sales office that took orders, and an order-processing department that saw to the subsequent details. The switchboard operator had to discover, and discover fast, which department to put people through to. She was therefore repeatedly asking callers: 'Are you placing an order or chasing an order?' It worked. At least it gave her the information she needed to direct the call accurately to the right department.

But did the company *want* every customer who telephoned to have it made so clear that orders *needed* chasing? I think not. Yet this is not untypical. There was efficiency at work here at one level, yet the overall effect was wrong. Who was at fault? The switchboard operator struggling to cope with the volume of calls? The manager supervising her? Or the sales or marketing department (who have final responsibility for customers)? The effect of similar efficiency, but coupled with the projection of a positive tone, would have been so much better. It is on the positive that we shall concentrate in what follows.

Certainly such things should not go by default. No organisation can afford to have inappropriate action taken simply because no one has thought about something, or not thought adequately about it.

Attention to detail is important here. Communication is never as straightforward as we sometimes believe, and the obvious voice-only nature of telephone communication compounds the problem. If something hits the wrong note or is simply unclear, then we cannot *see* a puzzled expression at the other end and may not so easily fine-tune an approach to correct matters and move on positively.

Like any communication, telephone contact must have a clear purpose. It is necessary to think before lifting the telephone to make a call – perhaps to plan and structure what will be done. Similarly it is essential that taking incoming calls is not viewed as entirely responsive. You cannot just lift the receiver and see what happens. We all need a clear idea of purpose:

● What is the call for?

■ What are the caller's expectations?

▲ What are we trying to achieve?

◉ What impression should we give?

◉ Exactly how must the call be handled: promptly, above all – or in order to project efficiency, or corporate or individual personality?

◉ What, as the receiver is replaced, should have been achieved?

So our objective here is to review the process to look at what can make this special kind of communication work for us, at the techniques involved, and at the skill with which the telephone must be handled.

An opportunity

Observation and experience suggest that, despite its importance, prevailing standards of telephone communication are not universally high. There are plenty of communication failures on the telephone; sometimes they constitute total derailment. Whenever this is the case there is an opportunity for those who get things right and for those who excel. It is one that demands no great cost or complication, just attention to detail and the appropriate deployment of the key techniques involved. The result can be powerful. Callers – including customers – find their expectations are not just met, but exceeded. Impressions are given that not only make the contact more pleasant and efficient but also enhance image and build business.

In the next chapter we review the essential principles of this special form of communication.

first principles 1

- *Brrr-brrr.*

- Hello?

Millions of times every day the telephone rings in offices all over the world. What happens next may be of greater or lesser significance, but it always matters. It may be a one-off contact or part of a series of contacts that gradually form a view of the organisation or person at the other end, but every time that ringing occurs it demands attention. Someone has to answer it, and that someone needs to deploy certain skills (as does the caller) if the contact is to work and be successful.

The switchboard

The first point of contact is often switchboard operators. Acting as invisible receptionists, they set the scene for the ensuing contact and must do so effectively. To be effective they must be organised. They need to know which calls go where, who does what, who backs up whom, and where priorities lie. Is it more important to obtain an outside number for the managing director or attend to an incoming customer enquiry? They need to know something about the outside world too. Who calls regularly? To whom do they speak? How well do they know us? Do they like to be recognised?

Operating the switchboard is no repetitive, parrot-like function. It is important to sound lively and interested and to act promptly and efficiently.

Key factors include:

● answering promptly

■ providing a friendly greeting such as 'Good morning'; by coming first this avoids anything crucial being missed (it can take the listener a moment to 'tune in' to the first words spoken)

▲ clearly identifying the organisation reached

● offering assistance: 'How may I help you?' ('may' is grammatically better than 'can', but such a phrase must be said carefully to avoid an insincere 'have-a-nice-day' sound).

Assistance must then be offered in a friendly and understandable manner. It is useful to think about the kind of question that will most easily identify where a call should go:

– Is this a first enquiry?

Once action is taken it must be efficient and accurate. People resent holding on for an age, unable to get back to the switchboard if an extension rings unanswered (although it should perhaps not do so), and alternatives must be offered helpfully:

- Can I get them to call you?

- Would you like me to find someone else who can help?

If there are delays, tell people exactly what is happening and always remember that time spent waiting on the telephone seems very much longer than it really is.

A good switchboard is a real asset to any organisation, acting moment by moment to build image and smooth communications.

Making a call may need some planning (see Chapter 5), but we now look at the need to respond appropriately when your telephone rings.

Taking a call

When the telephone rings you may not know who is calling, so you must always assume that the way you answer matters. If most of your calls are internal, you may be able to be a little more relaxed; if most are from customers, you should act accordingly. The basic rules include the following:

● *Answer promptly.*

■ *Identify yourself.* It may be sufficient to say your name. Stating your name in full sounds best, eg 'Mary Bolton.' You may prefer something longer: 'Good morning, this is Mary Bolton.' You may need something that includes a departmental or functional description: 'Good morning, sales office, Mary Bolton speaking.' This may, in part, be a matter of policy and consistency around a department and should correspond with whatever switchboard operators say if calls are coming via them.

▲ *Hold the telephone properly*. An obvious point, perhaps, but it really does impede hearing if the handset is tucked under the chin or pushed aside as you reach for something. You must be clearly audible.

● *Decide whether to take the call or not*. Some calls, eg from customers, may always need to be taken at once. But the telephone is obtrusive and, if you are busy, and a colleague simply wants a word, it may be acceptable to delay it: 'I'm just finishing an important draft: may I call you in half an hour?' Alternatively, the call may need to be transferred – something that must always be explained and handled promptly.

● *Adopt an appropriate manner*. This is not a question of insincerity or acting: it is just that we want to emphasise certain traits more with some people than with others – a nice, friendly (but not overfamiliar) tone with customers, say, and so on.

● *Speak clearly* (and a fraction slower than normal). Above all, don't gabble, and try to keep your thoughts organised: it is difficult to talk fluently the moment you pick up the receiver, not least because you cannot see the other person, and so thoughts can easily become jumbled.

■ *Signpost, if necessary.* Say something that tells the caller what is coming: 'Right, you want an update about the new brochure design project. Let me go through it. The key things are probably the costs, the copy and the design – and the timing. Now, first the costs…' This helps both parties, giving the caller the opportunity to amend the list and giving you a list to keep in mind (or even note down) and work through.

▲ *Always listen carefully.* The telephone may be a voice-only medium, but it is two-way. Don't do all the talking: make it clear you are listening by acknowledging points as you go along and make notes as necessary.

● *Be polite.* Of course, there could just be times when you *need* to shout at someone (at colleagues, if not customers)! More usually, though, it is important to maintain reasonable courtesies and, going by voice only, it can be easy to sound, say, abrupt when you are simply trying to be prompt.

● *Be aware of pauses.* If you say, 'Hold on a sec, I'll get the file', remember that the pause seems long to the person waiting. Sometimes it is better to suggest getting everything in front of you and phoning back. Or you can split what would otherwise seem a long pause into two, shorter, pauses by saying something like 'Right, I've got the file – I'll just turn to the figures you want.'

● *Have the right information to hand.* Many calls are routine. You can handle them more efficiently if you anticipate what information is needed and have it to hand (and in a form that is convenient to deal with on the telephone, eg papers in ringbinders lie flat and do not need a hand to hold them open when you are already trying to hold the receiver and write notes).

■ *Be careful about names.* People are sensitive about their names. Get them right – and do so early on: ask for the spelling or, if necessary, how to pronounce them, and use them occasionally during the conversation. It is annoying to outside callers if they have been asked their names by the switchboard operator, a secretary, and then the person who is handling the call only to be asked a fourth time, several minutes later, 'What was your name again?'

▲ *If necessary, call again.* Technically the telephone system is pretty good now, but if a bad line should really hinder communication it may be better to call again (nowadays there is also the problem of mobile phones fading away or cutting out as conditions, or perhaps location, change).

● *Hang up last.* Now you cannot both do this! But with something like a customer call, it is fine to be the first to bring the call to an end or simply to say 'Goodbye' (and not 'Bye-ee', incidentally). If it is you who put the phone down last it avoids the caller thinking of something else and feeling they have been left over-hastily.

Such a list could be extended and extended, no doubt; but the above captures the essentials and leaves space in this chapter for one other important basic point, to which we now turn.

Projecting the 'personal/corporate personality'

There is more to good telephone manner than just being polite and saying 'Good morning' as if you mean it. The general tone that you adopt sets the scene and gives people a clear impression of helpfulness and efficiency. But there are more powerful influences involved here.

People do not take such communication at face value: they read (or rather listen) between the lines. They ask themselves questions and believe that what they hear tacitly answers them. Who has not been surprised, on meeting someone known only over the telephone, to find that he or she is not at all as imagined? Such 'imagined' views can seem so clearly right.

People ask themselves 'What kind of person is this? Would I like to know them? What will they be like to deal with in future? Is what is happening so good that we make a note of their name and resolve to ask for them specifically next time?' Or is the projected image off-putting in some way? Does the person on the other end of the line make it all seem too much trouble, take a ridiculously long time, or not seem to know or be able to decide anything?

Both with internal and external contacts (those who know you and those who do not), the way you come over is vital: it matters to you and it matters to your organisation. Consider the internal ramifications first: the internal image.

Internal image

This is not the place for a treatise on your personal style. Suffice it to say, however, that what you do affects how you are seen. It is the same in other areas. For example, if someone looks a mess, has a desk that looks as if a bomb has hit it, and always misses every deadline set, then he or she may not seem the most promising choice for an interesting project or for promotion.

Just because you are not visible to your caller when you are speaking on the telephone does not mean that you are not sending out signals: you are. But you have some choice as to what those are. Do you want to come over as bright and efficient, or surly and unhelpful? How you act, what you say, and the way you use your voice – all influence the image you are projecting and are therefore worth considering. Give out the appropriate signs and you will feel the benefit over time.

External image

Here the implications are more complex, because people judge the organisation *through* you. They truly see you as personifying it. Action thus starts with clarity of purpose. How does your organisation want to be seen? This needs spelling out, and not simply in terms of 'good things' –

'efficient', 'high quality' etc – but in terms of values and feelings. Are you a caring, an innovative, or an exceptional organisation? If any of these, in what way?

Then you need to think about how this statement should be reflected in the manner that comes over on the telephone. For example, a caring company (in healthcare, say) must surely have time for people, so unseemly haste on the telephone may sit awkwardly with that image. Similarly, if your contacts are all at a high level, then some clear respect might be appropriate, whereas other business relationships may thrive on a chatty informality (while always remaining efficient).

A telephone 'handshake'

Overall, most of us do not like to deal at arm's length. We like to get to know people, especially if we are to deal with them regularly. On first meeting we are sometimes conscious of a drawing together as we begin to get the measure of people – shaking hands is part of such a relationship developing.

On the telephone it seems that things are, by definition, at arm's length. Perhaps it defines good telephone contact well when we are able to say that the style of the contact avoids this feeling. The person who makes you feel you know something about them, who comes over as likeable – and certainly as easy and pleasant to deal with – and who can, over time, create and maintain a real relationship is always a pleasure to speak with, whoever instigates the contact.

Whatever rules, principles, or good intentions there may be, the whole process of telephone communication depends on one thing: the voice and how it is used. It is to this that we turn in the next chapter.

By the way

What would you want if you had missed a call while reading this first chapter? A clear message, without a doubt. Messages are important; if one is lost it can cause chaos. The world is full of people puzzling over tiny bits of paper with indecipherable messages on them: 'BROWN (BROWNE?) RANG – TOLD HIM YOU WOULD CALL.' Which Brown? What did he want? How urgent was it? When did the message come in? Who took it? What's his number?

A good, clear message form is essential. It should be important-looking (some organisations have coloured message forms to stand out) and certainly be designed for taking and relaying to you *exactly* the information *you* want. On page 17 there is an example (which makes a nice distinction between 'action taken' and 'action promised'), but make sure that, whatever kind you use, it is tailored to work as you want.

Telephone message form

FOR: Name: Date:

               Department: Time:

From:

Name: Title:

Company:

Address:

Telephone: Fax:

About:

Action promised: Action taken:

Message taken by: ext:

making the voice work 2 for you

None of the techniques referred to so far works well without consideration of that most important element of telephone manner: the voice. Not only is the voice an important element, it has to act alone; by definition, telephone communication is voice-only. This makes for some difficulty. Try describing to someone how to, say, do up a necktie. You can *show* someone, but telling them is difficult, if not impossible.

The telephone does not help

The telephone is itself apt to make communication more difficult than it would be face to face. When we speak on the telephone, it distorts the voice somewhat (more so if there is a bad line): it seems to exaggerate the rate of speech and heighten the pitch.

Basics first: you must talk directly into the mouthpiece in a clear, normal voice (some women may need to pitch the voice somewhat lower than normal to avoid any squeakiness). It is surprising how many things can interfere with the simple process of speaking into the mouthpiece – for example:

- trying to hold a file open
- trying to write

▲ allowing others in the office to interrupt

● eating

● smoking.

All have an adverse effect. Some just need avoiding: don't eat or smoke when on the telephone! Others need organisation: as already stated, information in a ringbinder will lie flat and avoid the necessity of your trying to hold a file open, write, *and* hold the receiver. All it takes is a little thought and organisation to prevent such things diluting the effectiveness of your communication.

A wrong impression

One more point is worth noting before we get on to the positive aspects: the danger of humour or irony when you cannot visually judge the reaction. I am not suggesting that you become exclusively po-faced, but you do need to be careful. I remember the face of an aggrieved customer in a training film about the use of the telephone. Someone (less organised than he should be) is desperately trying to recall a name. 'Rolls, isn't it?' he says, and is corrected – 'Bentley.' An attempt at humour over the confusion of two names both used for cars clearly fails: it just makes matters worse.

Be doubly careful about anything that might be inappropriate for someone of a different ethnic origin from yourself, or who does not have a good command of English.

Exercise

Before we go on to review a plethora of factors affecting the voice, you might like to try the following. Get hold of a simple cassette player (or dictating machine). Choose something to say that you routinely deal with and record just a minute or two of your voice. Play it back. If you have not done anything similar for a while then you will notice at once that it does not sound like you. We all hear our own voice differently from the way it sounds to others. That *is* how you sound on the telephone. What do you think?

Reserve judgement and read on; you can check back later.

Voice and manner

Here, too, the details matter. All of the following, in no particular order of priority, are important.

Speak at a slightly slower rate than normal

You do not need to overdo this – slow down so much, that is, that you appear to be half-asleep. But pace is important. A measured pace is more likely to keep things clear and avoid misunderstandings. It allows the listener to keep up, particularly when, for example, he or she may be wanting to make a note: slow down especially for that.

In addition, too rapid-fire a delivery can sound glib and promote a lack of trust. It is important not to sound like a dodgy second-hand car dealer who will always go at a rate that precludes easy interruption.

Make inflection work for you

This is what makes, for example, a question mark stand out at the end of a sentence, and also what gives variety and interest to the way you speak. It is important that the intended inflection is noticed.

Smile

I do not mean that you should adopt a fixed grin. I mean that even though it cannot be seen, a pleasant smile produces a pleasant tone and this does make for the right sound. A warm tone of voice produces a feeling that the speaker is pleasant, efficient, helpful, and (most importantly) interested in the person at the other end of the line.

There are many situations (with customers, for instance) when enthusiasm is important. This has to be 'heard'; and it is about the only good thing that is contagious!

Get the emphasis right

It is necessary to get the emphasis right in terms both of individual words and the parts of the message that really count. In the first case, stress that '*This* is really important' or 'This is *really important.*' As for the second case – the part of the message to which the listener must pay most attention

– I can offer something of my own recent experience. I was struggling to note down a barrage of detail coming at me over the telephone when the person concerned suddenly said, 'The details don't really matter. When you come through to us next time just quote the following reference…That will get you through at once.' It would have been better to say that first.

Ensure clarity

It is no good sounding pleasant if what you say cannot be understood. Be clear and be particularly careful about names, numbers (you do not want to allow a 15 per cent discount to be confused with a 50 per cent one, for instance), and sounds that can be difficult to distinguish, such as 'f' and 's'. Just good, thoughtful articulation helps here.

An important detail is worth emphasising: find a way of doing it that works. For example, my post code ends 7BB, so over the telephone I always say, 'B for butter.'

Exercise some care if you have an accent (say, a regional accent). You have no reason to apologise for it, but may need to bear in mind that some elements of it will not be so clear to others as they are to you. Having said that, I find that some organisations favour the character that a regional accent can lend to a telephone transaction which may otherwise seem impersonal. The telephone banking organisation First Direct is one such: their research shows that callers are reassured by the north-country accents of some of their staff.

Be positive

This is especially important when an impression of efficiency is desired. Avoid saying 'possibly', 'maybe', and 'I think' when the expectation is that you should give definitive information. (Don't waffle, though: if you do not know, say so – you can always offer to get back to people.)

Be concise

Most of the people you speak with in a business context expect and appreciate it if you value their time. This means especially that convoluted descriptions should be thought about in advance; they should be made concise and precise.

Be careful with the social chat. It is often liked by regular contacts, but there can be a thin line between its being a pleasure to hear you again and your becoming a time-waster.

Avoid jargon

Jargon is professional shorthand and can be very useful – in its place. But you should be sure about what the other person understands and select the level of jargon to be used accordingly. Otherwise you can find that you are blinding people with science, as it were, and some – not wanting to appear foolish by asking – may allow meaning to be diluted.

For example, beware of company jargon (abbreviations of a department, process, or person); industry jargon (technical descriptions of products and processes); and even of general phrases that contain an agreed internal definition that is not

INSTITUTE OF PERSONNEL
AND DEVELOPMENT

Customer Satisfaction Survey

*We would be grateful if you could spend a few minutes answering these questions and return the postcard to IPD. <u>Please use a black pen to answer</u>. **If you would like to receive a free IPD pen, please include your name and address.***

....

1. Title of book ....

2. Date of purchase: month ....   year ....

3. How did you buy this book?
   ☐ Bookshop   ☐ Mail order   ☐ Exhibition

4. If ordered by mail, how long did it take to arrive:
   ☐ 1 week   ☐ 2 weeks   ☐ more than 2 weeks

5. Name of shop .... Town... Country ....

6. Please grade the following according to their influence on your purchasing decision with 1 as least influential: (please tick)

	1	2	3	4	5
Title					
Publisher					
Author					
Price					
Subject					

7. On a scale of 1 to 5 (with 1 as poor & 5 as excellent) please give your impressions of the book in terms of: (please tick)

	1	2	3	4	5
Cover design					
Page design					
Paper/print quality					
Good value for money					

8. Did you find the book:

   Covers the subject in sufficient depth   ☐ Yes   ☐ No
   Useful for your work   ☐ Yes   ☐ No

9. Are you using this book to help:
   ☐ In your work   ☐ Personal study   ☐ Both   ☐ Other (please state) ....

Please complete if you are using this as part of a course

10. Name of academic institution..

11. Name of course you are following? ....

12. Did you find this book relevant to the syllabus? ☐ Yes ☐ No   ☐ Don't know

Thank you!

2

Publishing Department

Institute of Personnel and Development

IPD House

Camp Road

Wimbledon

London

SW19 4BR

immediately apparent to an outsider, such as 'good delivery'. What is '24-hour service', other than insufficiently well defined? You can probably think of many more examples – perhaps some close to home!

Be descriptive

Good description can add powerfully to any message. There is all the difference in the world between saying that something is 'smooth as silk' and describing it as 'sort of shiny'. Things that are inherently difficult to describe can create a powerful impact if a well-thought-out description surprises by its eloquence. This is especially true of anything where the phraseology is not just clear but novel. For example, the sales executive of a hotel in which I was arranging a room for a training session described my chosen layout (a U-shape) as 'putting everyone in the front row'. Well said.

Conversely, beware of bland descriptions that impart minimal meaning. This means taking care not to describe a company's product as 'quite nice': what does that really mean? Similarly, 'user friendly' is nowadays so clichéd a phrase that it fails to differentiate one thing from another.

Use gestures

Yes, I know, they cannot be seen. But they may make a difference to how you sound, contributing to a suitable emphasis, for instance. Be careful, of course: you have to hang on to the phone and avoid knocking everything off the desk!

Adopt the right tone

In most circumstances you want to be friendly without being flippant, you want to sound courteous (*always* with customers), and you want to tailor your style to the circumstances, consciously deciding whether to evince a note of respect, a feeling of attention to detail, or whatever. Getting this right is what produces a good telephone 'handshake' feeling.

Sound yourself

To put it another way, be yourself. And certainly avoid adopting a separate, contrived 'telephone voice': it tends not to work and is difficult to sustain.

All these are things that can be consciously varied. Some – such as clarity – may need experiment, rehearsal, and practice. But together they combine to produce a satisfactory manner. The effect is cumulative, and this works both ways. It means that any shortfalls begin to add up, eventually diluting the overall power of what is done. Equally, the better you work in all these areas, the more the effects combine to create a satisfactory overall impression and style.

How your voice sounds goes logically with the way you use language, so we now turn to this heading.

Language

Several of the points above touch on language as much as voice – descriptiveness, for one. The point has also already been made that you should be yourself. So avoid 'officespeak'. A few examples are sufficient to illustrate what I mean.

Don't say:

- ● 'at this moment in time' (when you mean 'now')
- ◾ 'due to the fact that' (use 'because')
- ▲ 'I am inclined to the view that' (use 'I think').

And don't overdo the 'we': who is this corporate 'we', for goodness' sake? Make things personal: 'I shall ensure that...' sounds totally committed. Refer to people by name, if you can: 'Mary Brown in accounts will...' is much better than 'Someone...'.

Although grammatical perfection is not essential in conversation, it is good to avoid those things that are wrong and that irritate. For example, I spoke to someone the other day who kept adding to the word 'unique' by saying such things as 'very unique'. 'Unique' means 'one of a kind': you cannot have something that is 'very' one of a kind, so the intensifying word – the 'very' – is not needed. To add it is annoying, and therefore likely to detract from any good sense being talked.

Watch also for habits that can introduce an annoying or incorrect note: for example, ending every other sentence with 'right' or 'okay', or starting with a superfluous use of 'Basically'.

Listening

However well you speak and however well you get your point across, no telephone conversation should be a monologue. You need to generate feedback, and the first step to this is, not unnaturally, to listen. There is an old saying that people have two ears and one mouth for a good reason. Certainly, we should always remember that listening is just as important as speaking.

Good communication demands good listening skills, and this is especially vital on the telephone, when there are few other signs. Not only does it give you more information, others like it too. But you need to work at it. The following check-list shows how listening is an active process:

● *Want to listen*. This is easy once you take on board how useful it is.

■ *Sound like a good listener*. This comes through both language ('Tell me about…') and tone.

▲ *Strive to understand*. You need to 'read (or rather, hear) between the lines', not simply listen to the words (experience helps in this).

● *React*. Let people know you are listening by making small acknowledging comments: 'Right…Okay…Go on.'

● *Stop talking*. Remember, you cannot talk and listen at the same time, nor is it polite to try to do so.

● *Use empathy.* Put yourself in other people's shoes and make sure that you appreciate their point of view.

■ *Check.* Always check as you go along. Do not guess: if you are not sure what is meant, ask – and sooner rather than later.

▲ *Concentrate.* Don't let anything distract you (even in a busy office).

● *Note key points.* Always have paper and pencil in front of you when you talk on the telephone, so you can make notes. Sometimes it is not clear until later that certain points are important, and you do not want to keep saying, 'What was it you said about...?'

● *Don't let your mind wander.* It is easy to find yourself so busy trying to decide what to say next (for instance, how to rebut something) that you start to lose track of what is currently being said.

Good listening skills are a sound foundation for any sort of communication. On the telephone a distraction cannot be seen and your caller may not even realise that there is one. So another title in the *Management Shapers* series may be useful here: *Listening Skills* by Ian MacKay (2nd edn, revised by Krystyna Weinstein, IPD, 1995). Listening is important; we shall touch on it again here when we come to look at customer care and complaint-handling (respectively, Chapters 3 and 4).

Creating a dialogue

Two-way communication is not just a matter of two people talking one at a time and then listening in between. Creating a dialogue is something you need to work at actively. For example, you should:

- talk *with* people, not *at* them. It may help to form a mental picture of the person at the other end. Treating them purely as a disembodied voice is sure not to create the right impact.

- maintain a two-way flow. Don't interrupt, but do make sure, if the other person is talking at some length, that he or she is aware that you are still there and listening ('Right...'), and flag what you are going to do, in order to make your intentions clear ('Good, I have those details, so now perhaps I can just set out...').

- avoid jumping to conclusions – for whatever reason. It may be that you do know what is coming, but if you make unwarranted assumptions it can cause problems.

- give the feeling that things are being well handled. The dialogue should not just flow, it should actively appear to sort out or deal with things as necessary. The whole manner and structure of what is said should be purposeful and clarify whatever needs to be done to sort something out.

The people you speak to should feel that you want to talk to them, that you will let them have their say, and that you listen. At the same time there is a necessity in many conversations, from both parties' point of view, to keep calls short and businesslike.

Projecting the right image

Every time you pick up the telephone and speak someone will form an impression of you and, through you, of the organisation for which you work. This needs some thought. What do you *want* them to think of you? The answer depends on the person to whom you are speaking and the circumstances.

If you are talking to customers then there is quite a list of characteristics one doubtless wants to get over: courtesy, promptness, expertise, efficiency, good advice, and many more (see Chapter 3). But a similar situation in fact exists whoever it is you speak to, whether internal or external. This was touched on in the last chapter, so the point will not be revisited here except to say that the only channel to express whatever aspects are important here is the voice.

So, bearing in mind the general points about how you come over, we can move on to look at specific kinds of call. The most important calls that any organisation gets are those from their customers (although there may be people whom you want or need to regard as 'internal customers'). They all have to be handled just right if they are to be kept happy and satisfied, and if their business is to be confirmed or continue.

Chapter 3 reviews positive aspects of customer care and Chapter 4 the negative side – handling complaints. Before moving on, listen again to the recording that you made of yourself. What do you think now? Practice makes perfect, and more recording may help.

customer care

Most markets are competitive. Customers have plenty of choice and they do not *have to* do business with you. Their choice to do so is influenced by many things: the image and reputation of the organisation (in turn, influenced by advertising and a plethora of promotional techniques), the quality of the product or service you supply, guarantees, practice and policy, and more, such as – and it weighs heavily in the balance – people.

It is sometimes said of certain suppliers that they are 'good people to do business with'. It may be difficult to define such a statement, but people recognise the characteristics when they experience them. They want service to be good. This may be tangible: if something breaks down, the after-sales service cuts in and sorts the problem out quickly and efficiently. But it may also be less tangible. They want to be appropriately dealt with and they like it when customer-handling produces more than they expect, especially if they receive consistently excellent handling and the service that goes with it reaches similar standards.

Just the same process is involved with 'internal customers'. For example, an accounts or estimating department may be providing figures that another section – the sales office, say – is incorporating into information going to external customers. The service delivered internally affects directly that given down the line externally. It is worth thinking about just who your own 'internal' customers, if any, may be – and how to deal with them accordingly.

The effect of such things is cumulative. If you ask someone about a supplier they will probably be unable to recall for you the last contact they had with them: they are more likely to recall the feelings generated by a whole period of dealings with them. Yet that is made up of many different contacts using a variety of methods. Some of those contacts will doubtless have been on the telephone.

A significant difference

An example makes the point. Several times each year I do work in South East Asia. I tend to use the same airline and have a number of contacts with them each year. I always ask for the same member of their reservations team by name. Why? Such service is difficult to define, but I am recognised (sometimes after only a word or two and without giving my name). I get clear information. I feel that I can rely on what is done. The contact is polite, efficient, and friendly throughout. Nothing is too much trouble. The manner seems totally effortless and natural; and I like it. Yet I can hardly be their biggest customer.

One airline seat is much like another, so the effect of this is quite disproportionate. It matters. It matters a lot. And, in this case, it is a significant part of what keeps me going back again and again. Such an approach secures and builds business. It is clearly worth the effort – and there is, no doubt, an effort. This sort of thing does not just happen. Furthermore, I quote this having had only telephone contact with them. Their office may, for all I know, be chaos. My perception from their telephone performance is, however, of an efficient organisation that it is a pleasure to deal with.

Let us now consider what makes for good customer care from the point of view of the customer, and how these expectations can be met through effective telephone contact.

Overriding requirements

Customers want three things above all: prompt, efficient, and courteous service.

Prompt service

People hate waiting. They are impatient – all right, sometimes unreasonably impatient – but it is customers that we are concerned with here. Conversely they like being dealt with promptly; and they especially like it when the service is quicker than they expected.

The implications of this for telephone contact with customers include:

● being available at the right times (it is increasingly not tolerated if waiting times double at lunchtime, for instance, and more and more organisations are extending the hours in which they can be contacted in order to fit with their customers' lifestyles)

- ▪ answering the phone promptly (three rings should be enough)

- ▲ not keeping people waiting for information that they might reasonably expect you to have to hand

- ◉ not transferring callers around a department (with waits between) when something might reasonably be expected to be completed by one person.

Efficient service

This must reflect the nature of the particular business (and includes promptness):

- ◉ Information must be at hand (and be explicit, accurate, and appropriate).

- ▪ People must know what they are talking about.

- ▲ Policy and procedures must be customer-friendly (and this must be reflected in staff attitudes).

- ◉ Explanations must be clear, succinct, accurate, and fit the levels of experience or knowledge of customers.

- ◉ Advice must be provided as necessary and inspire confidence.

Courteous service

Customers are, well, customers. They see themselves as important and want to be treated accordingly. It is a golden rule *always* to be polite to customers, including the off-hand ones and even the rude ones. After all, coping with the difficult ones comes with the territory and, as the old saying has it, 'No customer is worse than no customer.'

Customers also see themselves as – and indeed are – individuals, and so again they want to be treated as such. Telephone contact that appears to be on 'automatic pilot', with the same words and sentiments ('Have a nice day!') trotted out to everyone, is not warmly welcomed.

Telephone contact will be seen as good customer care only if:

- interest in the customer is apparent and real
- respect is given
- normal courtesies are included ('please' and 'thank you')
- names are used (theirs and yours – and get theirs right!)
- more than the essential is being done.

In addition, *attitudes* are very important. Interest has been mentioned. Loyalty is also vital. It can change people's view of an organisation very quickly if staff are casting doubts on one another: 'I'll get back to you; our technical people never seem to do what they promise.' Overall, an attitude needs to exist – and be projected – of customer care, of someone who intends not only to be efficient and to satisfy the customer, but who enjoys doing so and gets satisfaction from succeeding at it.

Take the initiative

Although customers should not feel 'led by the nose', you should feel that any call, in-coming or out-going, is yours. You should direct it in order to make happen that which will meet your objectives and ensure that the customer feels that he or she is being suitably looked after.

The objectives of customer care are closely linked with sales. An enquiry may not result directly in an order (let us say a field salesperson must see the customer first and conduct a face-to-face meeting), but it should move the customer a step nearer to one. Whether it is a new prospect or an existing customer who we want to reorder, the objective is similar.

So, you run the kind of call that *you* want and that the customer finds that *he or she* likes (and preferably like better than any experience that that customer has had of the competition). This makes for a good maxim, and if you can become skilled at reading between the lines – assessing exactly what an individual customer wants and how you can handle him or her – so much the better.

A considered approach

The sequence of events necessarily varies, but certain principles always apply. Let us take an example of someone telephoning a travel agent about an overseas trip.

What are the customer's requirements? The trip may be business or pleasure; soon or far ahead; the customer may or may not know exactly where he or she wants to go. There will probably be concern about the cost and, possibly, bemusement as to the array of options. (It is a complex industry: I was recently quoted three prices that varied by more than 100 per cent for the same flight!) The customer will want advice and also service.

With all this in mind, consider this sequence of events:

● *Greeting.* If it is an in-coming call then the greeting is important. It should make clear the company reached, identify the person speaking by name, and also make clear who that person is (is he or she qualified to help, or has the tea-lady picked up the phone at a busy moment?) – and all this should be handled politely and quickly.

■ *Listen.* It is always crucial – throughout any transaction – to concentrate on what is being said (acknowledge and take notes). No customer will want to move on until sure that you appreciate what he or she wants. Customers expect you to listen carefully, expect to notice that you are doing so, and do *not* expect to have to repeat themselves unnecessarily.

▲ *Clarify.* Make sure that you have the requirement straight; check if necessary, and ask any supplementary questions that will fill out the picture. For this, open questions – which cannot be answered yes or no – are best: 'Tell me about the sort of hotel that you like.' For further details on the important skill of questioning see another *Management Shapers* title: *Asking Questions* by Ian MacKay (2nd edn, revised by Krystyna Weinstein, IPD, 1995).

● *Check that your response is satisfactory.* For example:

○ Should you deal with it or must it be (smoothly) transferred? ('I can help you best by putting you on to Mary: she deals with all our Far East work and is a real expert.')

□ What information can you begin to turn up? (This may require a brief pause: 'Just let me get that in front of me as we talk.')

● *Match your approach to the customer.* At least begin to do so, for example by acknowledging that he or she appears to be in a hurry and so dealing with things accordingly. (You may have to fine-tune your approach as you learn more about the customer.)

● *Make what you say add value.* In other words, make your side of the conversation *attractive* by stressing the advantages to the customer (as an individual and on the basis of what his or her needs appear to be); make it *convincing* by knowing the facts, offering proof, and believing in what you say; and, above all, make it *understandable* by speaking clearly, explaining things logically, and not overdoing the jargon.

Making things understandable is crucial. Many telephone conversations are spoiled because people become confused: they do not like to query things in case they seem foolish, and they end up putting the phone down convinced that this is not the organisation to deal with! Unexpected clarity scores points; customers love it if something they *expect* to be complicated is explained effortlessly.

On the telephone it is often best to concentrate on key issues rather than go for comprehensiveness. Too much information can become confusing and you cannot see how well the other party is taking it all in, or whether sheer volume is being read as pressure.

● *Maintain two-way communication.* Listen for when feedback is necessary, continue to ask questions to help you along, and be sure that the customer does not get the feeling of being swept along too fast.

■ *Check that your answer is satisfactory.* You should decide when to stop and make sure that you have given the customer what was wanted.

▲ *Sign off.* It is fine to be the first one to say 'Goodbye', but you should always be last to put the phone down (in case the caller has a further thought). Make sure that you handle any final administrative business or settle any future commitment before you finish ('So I shall ring you next month around the 20th to make an appointment for our technical people to visit') – and make any notes that are necessary.

Well executed, this customer care process is invaluable. It creates and develops business relationships, it acts as a foundation to sales activity, and it is good for image and profit.

The range of calls within the customer care category is broad. The above suits most situations, but to reinforce the points made and to act as a summary of certain key issues we shall end this chapter with a check-list. Always remember to:

◉ listen

▣ put yourself in the customer's shoes

▲ think about *what* you will say

◉ think about *how* you will express it

◉ try to anticipate the customer's reaction, and fine-tune your approach

◉ be polite (and patient) throughout

▣ 'engage the brain before the mouth' – always!

You may find that another book in the *Management Shapers* series, *Customer Care* by Frances and Roland Bee (IPD, 1995), usefully deals further with what has been touched on here.

handling complaints 4

Even the best-run organisations get some complaints. There may not be many (management action should ensure that) but, when they do come, they may be unexpected, and anyone who might have to pick up the telephone and deal with a complaint must know how to do so.

This is especially important for two reasons. First, the natural human reaction to complaints may actually make things worse – to claim defensively that 'It's not my fault.' If such a defensive attitude is struck then it is difficult to ensure a response that seems customer-sensitive. It may not be the direct fault of the person handling the matter; customers may not even care about whose fault it is – they just want things sorted out quickly, efficiently, and without fuss. Anything that smacks of evasion or hints at the 'It's not my fault' route will quickly just make matters worse. It intensifies the complaint, which then takes two forms: one of asking why something happened and wanting it sorted out, the other of wanting to know why it is not being handled better.

Secondly, prevailing standards of complaint-handling are perhaps not quite what they should be. We can all think of examples from our own experience, no doubt. As for myself, there was the time that the airline lost my luggage and could not even seem to…But I digress. It is, however, precisely because everyone *can* remember badly handled incidents that they come on strong when registering their complaint. They say, 'I want to speak to the manager', 'I demand to speak to the managing director', and even, I am told, 'I want to speak to a man'! They are simply trying to ensure that, this time, matters will get sorted out to their satisfaction.

Serious complaints may be more likely to get action than minor ones, but the fact is that they all matter. It is said – from some research – that if an organisation does something wrong, customers will tell 10 times the number of people as when they are impressed. So, it matters. And it is an opportunity.

We want to prevent complaints, sure, but if they have occurred then they should be seen as a positive opportunity to win back a customer. Indeed, if people think something has been really well handled – perhaps 'unexpectedly well' is how they would put it – then they may well be more likely to reorder than if grounds for a complaint had never arisen.

The nature of complaints

To handle them well, we have to understand something about them:

● *They are emotive.* As has been explained, customers are not just upset: they are determined to get satisfaction, and so feelings run high. After all, if failure to deliver some vital component has led to their entire production line grinding to a halt, then they are entitled to be aggrieved.

■ *Complaints have many causes.* Products, service activity, company policy and organisation, personal performance – all may be to blame, as may factors outside your direct control (an aeroplane delayed because of bad weather, perhaps). Some of these we can anticipate and this may help to handle them, eg if a production problem causes a quality failure then we can be ready for calls about items dispatched on the day it occurred.

▲ *Complaints may not always be justified.* The customer may be mistaken, so the immediate response should not always be to accept the blame.

● *Complaints are a source of information.* This may be important information, warning us to expect, or helping us to prevent, further complaints, or simply providing feedback about customer feeling. It is useful to have a dedicated form with which to document complaints. This is helpful in ensuring that no useful information is missed. (But don't let such forms be seen as a means of laying the blame, because this will hinder their use.) Such a form should be tailor-made to each organisation, but the example on page 48 may provide a guide.

With the proper approach (and assuming sound briefing) many complaints can be handled by whoever takes them without their having to be 'passed to management'. So how should complaints be approached?

Complaint form

To: .... Copies to: ☐ Production

.... ☐ Area manager

☐ Representative

☐ ....

Taken by: .... Date: .... Time: ....

Complainant's name: .... Position: ....

Company: ....

Address: ....

....

....

Tel. No.: ....

Nature of complaint: ....

....

....

....

ACTION

Action promised: | Action taken:

Follow-up action suggested: |

Here a systematic approach pays dividends. Of course, all complaints (like all customers) are individual, but most respond to a similar progression and procedure. On the telephone, there are seven stages:

1 Listen

No complaint can be properly handled unless you find out what has happened. So listen. Listen carefully and make it absolutely clear that you are prepared to listen. You may have heard it all before, but be very careful about jumping in and making wrong assumptions. Besides, people have a need to 'get it off their chests'. Listening sends out messages of sympathy and concern. It makes it clear that you want the facts, it shows that you are not instantly arguing (which the complainers may expect), and it gets the process off to a good start. (NB: if there are demands to 'speak to the manager', then listening may avoid this too. Sympathise but insist, politely, on getting the facts.) You could try saying:

- You may well need to speak to someone else, but I do need to know exactly what the problem is, so please, do tell me exactly what happened.

By the time the complainer has done that, provided your response to it is well handled, he or she may well have forgotten their earlier demand, which probably only meant: 'I want to talk to someone who will sort this out.'

Remember to show that you are listening with suitable brief comments, and be sure to get the detail, even if it means double-checking. It may also help if you make it clear that you are taking down notes.

2 Sympathise

This may well overlap with Stage 1 but often comes ahead of accepting blame (you may not yet know where the fault lies). You must make people feel that you are genuinely concerned that they should need to have this conversation, that you understand their point of view and can – really – put yourself in their shoes. Fake sincerity will always be detected, so you must take a real interest.

Show that there will be no argument, show that you will not interrupt, and apologise at least for the complainer's state of mind – 'I'm sorry you feel that way.'

Don't spout any of the stock phrases that simply get people even more wound up, eg 'This is the first time this has happened.' The response is likely to be along the lines of 'I don't care – it's happened to me – and I'm not sure I believe you anyway!' Similarly, don't refer to the fact that there have been 10 similar calls that morning. And move quickly on to:

3 Clarify

Precisely because complaints tend to be emotive, they can also be confusing. The detail comes tumbling out – 'and another thing…' – and it may therefore be difficult to follow.

It needs sorting out and the key aspects highlighting. Indeed, the ability to do this, and do it promptly and easily, is appreciated by the customer.

What is the best way to do this? Usually it is to summarise. You must say what you are doing:

- Right, let me summarise quickly to make sure I have this exactly right, then I shall see how we can help. What you are saying is…

Never use words like 'claim' (eg 'You claim that we lost your luggage') because this will provoke more argument just when the person may be calming down, having both got the matter off his or her chest and recognised that all seems to be being handled well. The ability to do this accurately and concisely is very valuable. You need your notes, your cool, and your wits about you.

At this point we can agree that we have the true picture, but it may be necessary to put matters – temporarily – on hold.

4 Check
This may only take a moment: one key pressed and the information is on screen in front of you. But it may take longer. Consider carefully the options. If you ask someone to hold on in the middle of registering a complaint, this had better not be for long. And if you promise to get back to the caller, then that is a promise that *must* be kept. Give yourself

sufficient time to check things and keep your promise, but make it seem a reasonable amount of time – 'I'll be back to you within the hour.'

Give people your name (if you did not do so on answering) so that they are reassured that you will not disappear forever and leave them unable to get back to you. State clearly what you will do and why:

> – I will talk to Mary Brown in accounts. She has the necessary records to hand. Once I have the details I will get back to you and we can sort things out. I'll call you by 10.30; is that convenient?

Once you have checked the circumstances, you can move on to the next stage.

5 Provide an answer

All the complainer wants is for things to be sorted out – and no hassle. You should recognise that turning the clock back is not an option. You can only make sure that whatever should have happened does so now, and try to compensate in some way for the fact that it did not happen earlier.

If the fault does not lie with the customer, then you must apologise unreservedly and say '*I am sorry.*' Remember that you speak for the company. It does not help to:

- lay the blame elsewhere ('It's those idiots in dispatch again')

- claim exception ('This has never happened before')

- make excuses ('We're very shortstaffed').

What is necessary is an open approach. A straightforward, personal, no-strings apology can clear the air and, together with any corrective action, can even be sufficient to make amends. Saying something like the following is likely to be most appropriate:

> – I am very sorry. This should never have happened, and I can see how annoying it must have been. Now let me...

Any action should be quick and convenient. For example, faulty goods might be collected or postage paid. It might be made to sound special: saying that you will lay on a special delivery might in fact only mean re-routing a van a few streets, but it implies a favour being done, because it provides good service.

Sometimes more than an apology and corrective action is necessary. You need to make some concession. It is a policy matter whether a delivery charge can be waived, an additional discount given, or whatever, but it helps if the person dealing with the complaint has the authority to make such decisions. Once someone says 'I shall go and see what's possible', the customer *knows* it is negotiable and the professional complainer (yes, there are some) will spend any time that he or she is left waiting on the line thinking of several more demands.

What if customers are at fault?

Let's say that they are complaining about late delivery and the docket shows clearly that the arrangement is not due for two more days. It is nice to let them down lightly – to save face. Don't say, 'Aha! It's not our fault.' You can still apologise, at least for the inconvenience they have suffered. Indeed, there may be lessons to learn:

- I'm sorry, it isn't due to be delivered until tomorrow. Do you have the docket there? The date is on the top right.

It may help if they see something like this and acknowledge it. You can encourage this – 'Do you have the docket there? You do? Let's have a look…' You might concede that it could be clearer, or offer to chase for quicker delivery anyway, but certainly you should end by making the customer feel that the query has been quickly checked and well dealt with – even if there was, in the event, nothing to complain about.

6 Follow through

Finally, follow through any corrective action that you have proposed. This might be administrative: 'I'll confirm the new details in writing.' If this is the case, be specific: if it will go in the post, first class, tonight, say so! Following through might simply be a question of forging a link with future contacts or orders:

- Do get on to me when you next order; I'll make sure everything is handled right. Or perhaps we can arrange a time for me to contact you?

A written apology, if things have been really bad, may be a necessary and appreciated touch. The objective, remember, is to deal with things in a way that confirms your organisation's continuing desirability as a future supplier.

7 Sign off
When all is done, you can end the call with a final note of apology and a link to the future – and let the caller put the telephone down first:

- Well, my apologies again, Mr. Jones, but that seems to have sorted things out – thank you for bearing with me. My name's Joan Dow, remember, and if I can help again just let me know. Goodbye.'

An opportunity

Overall, this is a vital kind of call. If it is not handled well it can make a bad situation worse and jeopardise future business and customer relationships. Handled well, it can not only build bridges, it can also heighten customer goodwill and make future business more likely.

One caveat: you cannot afford to be personally upset by complaints. Sometimes people are angry and rude, but dealing with such folk goes with the territory, as they say. If you keep your cool and handle matters systematically, then complaint calls – of which there should not be very many – can be handled smoothly.

Now, finally, we turn to some other special applications of telephone skills.

special intentions 5

Many calls have a special purpose. Some of those, as we shall see, require additional skills. But all calls need some degree of planning. This may be just a moment's thought or may demand something more formal – a discussion with a colleague, a few minutes, and a few points noted down which you can have in front of you as you subsequently speak.

Whatever is necessary, a key part of it is to set your objectives: what are you trying to achieve? Without that clearly in mind, you may be reduced to 'making it up as you go along'. To some extent, of course, you do have to improvise, but you tend to do so far better if you are working from some sort of plan.

A route map

A useful analogy here is that of a route map. If you plan to make a journey, one where you are unfamiliar with the route, it is sensible to check the map first. You check the best route that you can take. But this does not need to act as a straitjacket to the extent that any deviation from the route is impossible. Indeed, if you hit roadworks or a stretch of road where there has been an accident, then having the mental picture provided by the map allows you to divert more easily from your planned route and work your way around the obstruction.

So it is with a telephone call. You form an objective, you know what you intend to achieve, and you work out – broadly at least (I am not suggesting scripting anything!) – how you want to run the conversation. But it *is* a conversation. It is two way, and it is not totally predictable. Whoever you are speaking with will not speak, ask questions, or react exactly as you hope: there will quite possibly be 'roadworks'.

Conducting a successful telephone conversation is thus dependent on not only what you prepare but also on your ability to adapt, improvise, and work with the circumstances you find *en route*.

Objective and manner

If you are clear about what you want to achieve, then this will not only assist in framing the conversation and deciding the logic, sequence, and content of what you say but it will also provide an indication as to the manner in which you say it.

For example, a call that involves, say, explaining an administrative process should be clear and logical. It might contain a request for the other person to get a form in front of them (so that despite the voice-only restriction, you can both look at something together), followed with a stage-by-stage explanation of what should be done first, second, and so on. Such explanation is assisted if the manner in which you speak appears helpful, unhurried ('Let's get this right!'), and is clearly concerned with the detail.

This is true of any telephone call. A complaint should be made with certainty and clout. The response to it should be sympathetic and efficient. A call that answers a customer enquiry should, among other things, express interest in that customer and give the impression of an individual approach in the way it is handled.

Yet some calls present special challenges. The following makes a good example.

Calls that must be handled assertively

Sometimes the handling process needs extra clout. Assertiveness is the topic of another title in this series (see *Assertiveness Skills* by Terry Gillen, IPD, 1997), so instead of going into all the techniques involved we shall take just one or two examples. Because telephone calls may be about anything, from matters of staff discipline to cajoling people to hit their deadlines, there are many examples. One that every organisation has to deal with sometimes is the call made to debtors.

Despite the fact that the vast majority of customers do actually expect to pay for what they get, this can be an awkward – perhaps embarrassing – kind of call to make. The objective is clear: a cheque in the post – and promptly. What does this say about the manner that you should adopt? Realistically we must expect that some people are always looking for any excuse to delay payment. A circumspect approach is hardly suitable in such circumstances: 'I'm sorry to worry you, but I wonder if maybe…' Something more assertive is called for: 'I felt I had to call you: I'm looking at an invoice here that is three months overdue. I'm sure you…'

If this seems difficult to do, here is a tip – and don't laugh: this is tried and tested! It really works. Make the call standing up. You may be surprised how this affects your state of mind and your ability to come on a bit stronger. It could be useful for more than collecting debts. And, of course, no one will know whether you are sitting or standing. Well, people in your office may notice; so be it, but the person whom you are calling does not. He or she will simply think of you as being more of a force to be reckoned with; and in the end all that matters is that the bill is settled.

When such assertiveness is necessary, then additional thought before picking up the phone makes good sense. Experiment, and when you find an approach that works for you (preferably without upsetting people!) stick with it. Too much circumspection may be costly if you do not achieve your purpose.

Horses for courses

As the above example makes clear, the trick here is to put thinking first. What is the objective? What is necessary to achieve it? And what – in light of that – is the best way of going about it? These tactics provide guidance every time.

Consider another example: making calls to check your company's service standards. Maybe you have a short questionnaire to complete. So, what is the objective? – To get people to spend long enough talking to you to get the questionnaire completed and allow you to analyse the information collected. The first job then is to persuade them to talk. Tell people that responding to the questionnaire would be useful (to them personally and others), that it will not take long (quoting a time may help), that it is easy to do (no convoluted questions), and that it is a chance for them to have their say. If they agree, then your manner has to reflect the promises. You should seem to be cracking through the questionnaire with an eye on the respondents' time, yet remain friendly and appreciative.

Every case yields to this kind of thinking. One further special application is worth a separate word.

Persuasive calls

Many business situations call for some persuasion. Telephone selling may conjure up a vision of sophisticated approaches or simple customer contact, but you do not have to be involved in selling to need to be persuasive. Trying to get agreement to shift a deadline, miss a meeting, or have an extra week's holiday may all require similar techniques.

So, it is worth noting the main differences involved when a persuasive, or sales, call is being made. All the fundamental skills of using the telephone remain relevant and must be deployed. But more than that is necessary – too much more to give a complete rundown on such techniques here, but there are four main stages:

1 Opening

First impressions last, and are doubly important if we are not just trying to give people a good impression, but persuading them to take action. It is particularly important here to:

- get off to a good, confident start

- begin to establish rapport

- make it clear that you understand the customer's situation

- ask questions to discover what the customer might want (good, accurate, need-identification is crucial, making everything else that follows more certain).

2 Presentation

This is the core of our call, when we make the case for the action that we intend to prompt (people weigh up the case and want to consider the pros and cons). To be persuasive, your presentation of your case must be:

- *understandable*. No customer will ever agree to, or buy, anything if the details about it are difficult to follow, especially if he or she thinks that it should not be complicated.

■ *attractive*. This is the heartland of persuasive technique: setting out the benefits (what the action or product or service will do for, or mean to, people) rather than just the facts.

▲ *convincing*. Here additional proof may be necessary; after all, why should the person on the other end of the line believe everything that someone with an axe to grind says?

3 Handling objections

People do not – usually – just say yes because they are asked to agree. They often have reservations or queries; they may object that what is being offered is not value for money, or is simply not for them. They feel that too much compromise is involved. Such comments have to be dealt with and a favourable picture maintained.

4 Closing

It is inherent to selling that we must at a certain point actually ask for the order. Indeed, any agreement needs to be prompted. Closing does not by itself cause people to agree to make an order for a service or product (everything else that is done and the interest thus generated do that). Rather, it converts interest into action. The action may be actually to make an agreement or purchase, or it may involve a commitment *en route*, for example agreement to a sales meeting.

The best definition of selling is that it is 'helping people to buy'. It is not something you can 'do to people'. It involves two-way communication that helps a choice to be made and ensures that people's needs are met. On the telephone, without the credibility and trust that face-to-face contact can inject, all the techniques outlined above are very important.

Whether you are involved in simple customer contact, more specialised telephone selling, or just want to gain agreement from a colleague and so must act persuasively, remember that this takes you into a separate dimension of communication skills. Never assume that it is straightforward – and look more closely into the skills involved if this would be useful.

afterword

If one thing has been made clear in the preceding pages, it is that the telephone cannot – must not – be taken for granted. Its influence is considerable: whenever people answer the telephone or make a call someone else is 'reading between the lines'. What sort of person is this? What kind of organisation does he or she represent? Is this contact going to be useful, easy, worthwhile – or is it going to cause confusion and frustration?

The signs are given and received very quickly, and perception is what matters. Someone failing to get a point across may have good intentions, may be really trying...but end up being just that – trying. What is more, the power of such impressions is awesome.

The dangers

Consider: someone rings his or her bank. It is, maybe, a simple matter of checking some detail, but the caller ends up being passed from pillar to post, several people picking up the call yet failing either to provide the relevant information or to pass the call on to someone who can – or failing even to apologise for the muddle. The caller loses patience, says 'It doesn't matter', and rings off.

A week later the bank receives a letter closing a significant company account. And no doubt someone asks, 'Whyever are they doing that?'

Ultimately, poor telephone skills are equated with poor business and service skills. They do more than ruffle feathers, upset people, and turn routine matters into complaints or arguments: at worst, they lose business.

The opportunities

It is in fact fortuitous that there is still much poor practice in this area, because it makes it comparatively easy to shine. Good practice is clearly very important with customers and can create, maintain, and develop customer relationships and the business they bring. Exceeding expectations (or industry standards, perhaps) can do still more. But good telephone skills are important across the board, internally and externally, whomever calls are made to or taken from. Good skills can:

- save time
- save money
- ensure clear communication
- reduce hassle and frustration
- create a positive image (of people and organisations)
- improve motivation

and more. People and their communication with one another are inherent to the business process. Take away either and there is not much left. It is all too easy to regard the telephone as much as an interruption and an inconvenience as an asset. Without consideration it will be 'just another telephone call'. Given thought and deploying the right skills it can be a real asset, one that works day by day, again and again, to produce a positive effect...

- *Brrr-brrr.*

- Hello? – No, not now, I'm busy – writing that thing about telephone skills – call me later...Bye.

...provided that we all remember, at all times.

With over 100,000 members, the **Institute of Personnel and Development** is the largest organisation in Europe dealing with the management and development of people. The IPD operates its own publishing unit, producing books and research reports for human resource practitioners, students, and general managers charged with people-management responsibilities.

Currently there are some 160 titles covering the full range of personnel and development issues. The books have been commissioned from leading experts in the field and are packed with the latest information and guidance on best practice.

For free copies of the IPD Books Catalogue, please contact the publishing department:

Tel.: 020-8263 3387
Fax: 020-8263 3850
E-mail: publish@ipd.co.uk
Web: www.ipd.co.uk/publishing

Orders for books should be sent to:

Plymbridge Distributors
Estover
Plymouth
Devon
PL6 7PZ

(Credit card orders) Tel.: 01752 202 301
Fax: 01752 202 333

Upcoming titles in the *Management Shapers* series

Publication: April 2000

Conquer Your Stress
Cary L Cooper and Stephen Palmer
ISBN 0 85292 853 X

Managing for the First Time
Cherry Mill
ISBN 0 85292 858 0

Transforming Your Workplace
Adryan Bell
ISBN 0 85292 856 4

Other titles in the *Management Shapers* series

All titles are priced at £5.95 (£5.36 to IPD members)

The Appraisal Discussion

Terry Gillen

Shows you how to make appraisal a productive and motivating experience for all levels of performer. It includes:

- assessing performance fairly and accurately

- using feedback to improve performance

- handling reluctant appraisees and avoiding bias

- agreeing future objectives

- identifying development needs.

1998 96 pages   ISBN 0 85292 751 7

Asking Questions

Ian MacKay

(Second Edition)

Will help you ask the 'right' questions, using the correct form to elicit a useful response. All managers need to hone their questioning skills, whether interviewing, appraising or simply exchanging ideas. This book offers guidance and helpful advice on:

● using various forms of open question – including probing, simple interrogative, opinion-seeking, hypothetical, extension and precision etc

■ encouraging and drawing out speakers through supportive statements and interjections

▲ establishing specific facts through closed or 'direct' approaches

● avoiding counter-productive questions

● using questions in a training context.

1998 96 pages   ISBN 0 85292 768 1

Assertiveness

Terry Gillen

Will help you feel naturally confident, enjoy the respect of others and easily establish productive working relationships, even with 'awkward' people. It covers:

- understanding why you behave as you do and, when that behaviour is counter-productive, knowing what to do about it

- understanding other people better

- keeping your emotions under control

- preventing others' bullying, flattering or manipulating you

- acquiring easy-to-learn techniques that you can use immediately

- developing your personal assertiveness strategy.

1998 96 pages   ISBN 0 85292 769 X

Constructive Feedback

Roland and Frances Bee

Practical advice on when to give feedback, how best to give it, and how to receive and use feedback yourself. It includes:

- using feedback in coaching, training, and team motivation

- distinguishing between criticism and feedback

- 10 tools for giving constructive feedback

- dealing with challenging situations and people.

1998 96 pages   ISBN 0 85292 752 5

The Disciplinary Interview

Alan Fowler

This book will ensure that you adopt the correct procedures, conduct productive interviews and manage the outcome with confidence. It includes:

- understanding the legal implications

- investigating the facts and presenting the management case

- probing the employee's case and defusing conflict

- distinguishing between conduct and competence

- weighing up the alternatives to dismissal.

1998 96 pages   ISBN 0 85292 753 3

Leadership Skills

John Adair

Will give you confidence and guide and inspire you on your journey from being an effective manager to becoming a leader of excellence. Acknowledged as a world authority on leadership, Adair offers stimulating insights into:

- recognising and developing your leadership qualities

- acquiring the personal authority to give positive direction and the flexibility to embrace change

- acting on the key interacting needs – to achieve your task, build your team, and develop its members

- transforming the core leadership functions such as planning, communicating and motivating into practical skills you can master.

1998 96 pages   ISBN 0 85292 764 9

Listening Skills

Ian MacKay

(Second Edition)

Improve your ability in this crucial management skill! Clear explanations will help you:

- recognise the inhibitors to listening

- listen to what is really being said by analysing and evaluating the message

- interpret tone of voice and non-verbal signals.

1998 80 pages   ISBN 0 85292 754 1

Making Meetings Work

Patrick Forsyth

Will maximise your time (both before and during meetings), clarify your aims, improve your own and others' performance and make the whole process rewarding and productive. The book is full of practical tips and advice on:

- drawing up objectives and setting realistic agendas

- deciding the who, where, and when to meet

- chairing effectively – encouraging discussion, creativity and sound decision-making

- sharpening your skills of observation, listening and questioning to get your points across

- dealing with problem participants

- handling the follow-up – turning decisions into action.

1998 96 pages   ISBN 0 85292 765 7

Motivating People

Iain Maitland

Will help you maximise individual and team skills to achieve personal, departmental and, above all, organisational goals. It provides practical insights into:

- becoming a better leader and coordinating winning teams

- identifying, setting and communicating achievable targets

- empowering others through simple job improvement techniques

- encouraging self-development, defining training needs and providing helpful assessment

- ensuring that pay and workplace conditions make a positive contribution to satisfaction and commitment.

1998 96 pages   ISBN 0 85292 766 5

Negotiating, Persuading and Influencing

Alan Fowler

Develop the skills you need to manage your staff effectively, bargain successfully with colleagues or deal tactfully with superiors. Sound advice on:

- probing and questioning techniques

- timing your tactics and using adjournments

- conceding and compromising to find common ground

- resisting manipulative ploys

- securing and implementing agreement.

1998 96 pages   ISBN 085292 755 X

Working in Teams

Alison Hardingham

Looks at teamworking from the inside. It will give you valuable insights into how you can make a more positive and effective contribution – as team member or team leader – to ensure that your team works together and achieves together. Clear and practical guidelines are given on:

- understanding the nature and make-up of teams

- finding out if your team is on track

- overcoming the most common teamworking problems

- recognising your own strengths and weaknesses as a team member

- giving teams the tools, techniques and organisational support they need.

1998 96 pages   ISBN 0 85292 767 3